STOCK CARS

BY THOMAS K. ADAMSON

BELLWETHER MEDIA • MINNEAPOLIS, MN

EPIC BOOKS are no ordinary books. They burst with intense action, high-speed heroics, and shadows of the unknown. Are you ready for an Epic adventure?

This edition first published in 2019 by Bellwether Media, Inc.

No part of this publication may be reproduced in whole or in part without written permission of the publisher. For information regarding permission, write to Bellwether Media, Inc., Attention: Permissions Department, 6012 Blue Circle Drive, Minnetonka, MN 55343.

Library of Congress Cataloging-in-Publication Data

Names: Adamson, Thomas K., 1970- author.
Title: Stock Cars / by Thomas K. Adamson.
Description: Minneapolis, MN : Bellwether Media, Inc., 2019. | Series: Epic: Full Throttle | Includes bibliographical references and index. | Audience: Age: 7-12.
Identifiers: LCCN 2018002173 (print) | LCCN 2018002785 (ebook) | ISBN 9781626178762 (hardcover : alk. paper) | ISBN 9781681036236 (ebook)
Subjects: LCSH: Stock cars (Automobiles)–Juvenile literature.
Classification: LCC TL236.28 (ebook) | LCC TL236.28 .A33 2019 (print) | DDC 629.228/5–dc23
LC record available at https://lccn.loc.gov/2018002173

Editor: Christina Leaf   Designer: Jeffrey Kollock

Printed in the United States of America, North Mankato, MN

TABLE OF CONTENTS

Stock cars roar down the track. With two laps to go, the car in second place darts to the inside. The top cars race side by side.

The second-place car suddenly shoots ahead! On the final turn, the new leader weaves back and forth. No one can pass him!

DRAFTING FOR SPEED

Stock cars may race inches behind another car. This is called drafting. It helps cars gain more speed than a single car.

He speeds across the finish line. The winner!

WHAT ARE STOCK CARS?

Stock cars look like regular passenger cars. But they are specially made for racing. Stock cars race on **speedways**, short tracks, and road courses. **NASCAR** races are among the most popular.

speedway

STICKERS

Stock cars are covered with company logos. Companies pay for these ads to sell more products.

Stock car races are up to 600 miles (966 kilometers) long. Drivers speed around the track for many laps.

At some tracks, they race at over
200 miles (322 kilometers) per hour!

THE HISTORY OF STOCK CARS

Racing cars was popular in the 1940s. People **modified** their cars to be faster. NASCAR organized in 1947 to make sure different tracks had fair rules. Many of these early races were held on dirt tracks.

Daytona Beach course

North Wilkesboro Speedway

13

STOCK CAR TIMELINE

1959

Lee Petty wins the first Daytona 500

1950

The first paved NASCAR speedway opens in Darlington, South Carolina

1948

First NASCAR race is held on a beach road course in Daytona Beach, Florida

1969

The largest superspeedway, Talladega, opens in Alabama

2010

Jimmie Johnson wins a record fifth championship in a row

NASCAR races became popular quickly. Now, stock cars race on paved tracks in huge **stadiums**. Drivers use cars made just for racing. Stock car styles have changed, but the goal has not. Drive fast and finish first!

STOCK CAR PARTS

Stock car tires have no **tread**. This gives them more grip on dry tracks. The **spoiler** helps push the car downward for better control at high speed.

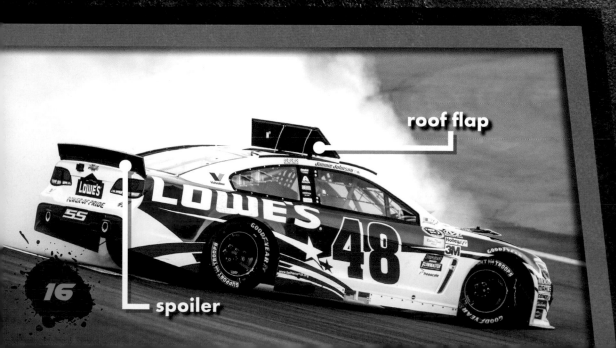

roof flap

spoiler

FAKE HEADLIGHTS

The headlights on stock cars are stickers! These help make the cars look more like passenger cars.

When a car loses control, roof flaps pop up. They keep the car on the ground.

CLIMB IN

Stock cars do not have doors. The driver climbs in through the window.

HANS

Many parts protect drivers in crashes. The driver is surrounded by steel tubing called a **roll cage**. A helmet and head-and-neck restraint system (HANS) protect the driver's head. A window net shields the driver from **debris**.

IDENTIFY A STOCK CAR

roof flaps

window net

spoiler

roll cage

smooth tires

STOCK CAR COMPETITIONS

THE SUPER BOWL OF RACING

The biggest stock car race of the year is the Daytona 500.

2016 Daytona 500

NASCAR races are the biggest stock car events. During races, pit crews change tires at **pit stops**. They keep the fuel tank full. Drivers compete in regular season and **playoff** races. The fastest car wins!

pit stop

GLOSSARY

debris—the pieces of something that has been broken or destroyed

modified—changed to meet a specific need

NASCAR—short for the National Association for Stock Car Auto Racing; NASCAR organizes stock car races in the United States.

pit stops—short breaks when race cars stop for fuel, new tires, and quick repairs

playoff—related to a series of contests after a regular season ends to determine a championship

roll cage—a strong steel frame inside a stock car that surrounds and protects the driver

speedways—paved racetracks for stock car racing; speedways are often in the shape of an oval.

spoiler—the part that sticks up on the back of a stock car that helps push the car down onto the track for better control

stadiums—big buildings that have a large open area surrounded by seats; stadiums host large sports games, concerts, and other events.

stock—the regular model of something; stock cars are made to look like regular models of cars people can buy.

tread—the ridges on a car tire that help it keep from slipping when the road is wet

TO LEARN MORE

AT THE LIBRARY

Long, Dustin. *NASCAR Racing.* Minneapolis, Minn.: SportsZone, 2015.

Mikoley, Kate. *NASCAR: Stats, Facts, and Figures.* New York, N.Y.: Gareth Stevens, 2018.

Phillips, H. *Inside a Stock Car.* New York, N.Y.: Cavendish Square, 2015.

ON THE WEB

Learning more about stock cars is as easy as 1, 2, 3.

1. Go to www.factsurfer.com.

2. Enter "stock cars" into the search box.

3. Click the "Surf" button and you will see a list of related web sites.

With factsurfer.com, finding more information is just a click away.

INDEX

The images in this book are reproduced through the courtesy of: action sports, front cover, pp. 1, 8-9, 10, 14-15, 19 (Dewalt car); Icon Sportswire/ Getty Images, pp. 4-5, 6; Chris Graythen/ Getty Images, p. 7; Action Sports Photography, pp. 8, 11, 16, 18-19, 20-21, 21; RacingOne/ Getty Images, pp. 12, 12-13, 14 (Lee Petty), 15 (Talladega); Miami Herald/ Getty Images, p. 15 (Jimmie Johnson); Doug James, pp. 16-17; PhotoMDP, p. 19 (roll cage); Matthew Jacques, p. 19 (tires).